The Curse of Time

Christian A. Dickinson

Title: *The Curse of Time*
Subtitle: *Time Began When Eternity Broke*
Written by: Christian A. Dickinson
Illustrations by: Learning Engineered LLC
Published by: Learning Engineered Publishing

Library of Congress Control Number: 2025942264
ISBN (Print): 978-1-965741-40-5

First Edition: 2025

Printed & Created in: United States of America
Text and Illustration Copyright © 2025

Learning Engineered Publishing is a division of Learning Engineered LLC and a subsidiary of Carpe Diem Unlimited Holdings, Inc.

LEARNING ENGINEERED
PUBLISHING

Contents

Dedication

To my Lord Jesus Christ,
who shattered the curse of time at the
cross
and ushered in the eternal now of the
Kingdom of the Gospel.

To my brother in Christ and dear friend
Nick,
whose friendship helped me connect the
dots.

Preface: Why I Wrote This Book

I didn't aim to write a theology of time. I wrote a testimony—sparked at thirteen when time fractured while fishing (p. 7). As I wrote, a hunger surfaced: for peace beyond circumstance, a stillness found only in God's eternal now.

Too many believers, worn thin by anxiety, are trapped in *chronos*—time's ticking tyranny. But *kairos*—God's eternal now—offers freedom.

Dallas Willard, facing death, said, "I think that when I die, it might be some time until I know it" (*The Allure of Gentleness*, 2015). His peace, rooted in God's presence, is what I glimpsed.

I invite you: trade *chronos's* pressure for Jesus' Kingdom (John 17:3, ESV). Salvation is complete

surrender—knowing Jesus and living His Kingdom today.

Rest in kairos.

Prologue: Connecting the Dots

This book didn't begin as a theory. It began as a moment—one that didn't fit inside time.

I was thirteen, standing atop a forty-foot embankment behind our house, fishing rod in hand, muttering to God, "Just one fish." The canal had been quiet all day—empty, dead. Then, suddenly, I wasn't there anymore.

I was taken—lifted, shown. Not a voice, not a dream. A vision. I saw myself. My future self, standing right there, casting the line into the water, reeling it in—hook set, fish caught. And then I was back. Back in my own moment, back in my body, but everything had changed. I scrambled down the embankment and did exactly what I had seen. Cast. Set. Snap! A large-mouth bass, just like in the vision.

It wasn't about the fish.

When I ran home, breathless and stumbling over my words, my father looked at me, eyes soft with recognition. "You experienced the presence of the Lord," he said. "The fish? That was just the cherry on top."

He was right. Something had pierced through time—kairos breaking into chronos—and it marked me.

But I didn't yet have words for it. Not until years later. Not until Nick.

I met Nick in 2005. He wasn't just a colleague—he became the epicenter of a two-decade journey. He had a way of pulling on threads I didn't know were loose. We talked about heaven, about the gospel of the Kingdom, about things most people are too cautious to say out loud. Not to form a theology, but to bear witness.

He handed me a book once—about a man who had cursed God, died from a box jellyfish sting, and began slipping away from a distant light. As the light faded, so did everything human: peace, belonging, love. Fear crept in. In desperation, the man cried out, "Jesus, Jesus, Jesus!"—and he was pulled back to life.

He'd died. He'd been legally gone. But grace met him in another time, in God's time.

That testimony shattered my categories. Grace wasn't just deep—it was timeless.

Another dot. Nick and his wife took in a baby from Africa—born with massive heart issues, not expected to live. He wasn't their son at first. Just a child they'd agreed to care for. But he became family.

The first time I met Momo, Nick was rocking him on a small porch. I approached, unprepared for what I felt. The presence of the Lord settled on that place.

Not metaphor.

Not emotion.

Holiness.

Holy ground.

Nick asked if I wanted to hold him. I couldn't. "I'm not worthy," I said. Because I wasn't. Not then.

This boy wasn't just sick—he was sacred. He lived in our time, but he didn't seem bound by it. He was being carried by the mercy of a God who moves above the clock.

Then came another dot—a podcast episode shared by Nick. A man, dead for 44 hours, describing heaven. What made his story different wasn't just what he saw—it was how clearly he remembered everything. The way he described it... I'd been there. Twice. Once alone. Once with my wife. I've never shared those stories. Maybe someday. But what he described confirmed what I already knew:

Chronos and kairos are not metaphors. They're realms.

And only one of them has the power to heal.

For twenty years, I collected these moments like dots on a page. Not the kind where you can already see the picture before you start—the good ones. The ones where the image only emerges *after* every line has been drawn. And when I finally saw it...I saw it all.

Time as curse.

Eternity as gift.

Jesus as the one who cast the line.

This book is that picture.

It's for thinkers, for skeptics, for seekers. For theologians and teachers, but also for tired parents, wondering souls, and anyone who's ever whispered, "Just one fish, Lord."

Let's connect the dots.

Chapter 1

In the Beginning, There Was No Time

Picture Eden as a river of God's peace, its current unbroken by the clamor of clocks. Genesis 1 unveils a world free from decay: God's voice summoned light, His Spirit hovered over chaos, and creation bloomed in rhythms of beauty (Genesis 1:1–3, ESV). Adam and Eve named animals, tended the garden, and walked with God in the cool of the day, their hearts untouched by time's rush (Genesis 2:15, ESV). This was kairos (καιρός, God's appointed, time-less moment), where past and future vanish into His eternal presence. Not chronos (χρόνος, sequential time), the relentless chain of hours that governs our days with deadlines, decay, and loss, binding us to the fleeting rhythms of earthly existence (Ecclesiastes 3:1–8, ESV).

I believe Eden was God's now—a paradise where aging held no power. But was time part of His design—or the shadow of a fracture we've yet to uncover? This chapter begins our journey by asking: Did God create time, or did sin's echo start its countdown?

Eden's Song

Genesis 1's "days" weren't a stopwatch's tally but a divine symphony. The Hebrew yom (,יֹום day) can mean a day, an era, or God's creative act, as Philo (c. 20-50 CE) taught. No sun or moon shone until Day Four (Genesis 1:14, ESV), so God's light alone marked "evening and morning" (Genesis 1:5, ESV). These were rhythms of worship, not schedules.

The "seasons" of Genesis 1:14, from the Hebrew mo'ed (,מֹועֵד sacred times or divine appointments), meant holy feasts, not calendars, as Basil of Caesarea (c. 370) noted. Eden's time was a song of peace—God's now in every breath. Adam and Eve lived in harmony; in their days, they were in a dance of communion, free from anxiety or decay.

As a boy, I'd sit on our porch as my father spoke of God's presence, his voice steady against the evening hum of crickets. "The Lord's nearness," he'd say, "is like Eden's air—time fades, and only He remains." Those words stirred my young heart, painting a peace beyond clocks.

Yet something broke Eden's song. Could an angelic rebellion, hinted at in scriptures like Isaiah 14, as we'll explore, have cast a shadow over paradise?

God Beyond Time

Scripture sings, "From everlasting to everlasting, you are God" (Psalm 90:2, ESV). Augustine (397-400) saw God's eternity as a single "Today," holding all moments as one. Lewis (1964) called it the "eternal now," unbound by our "time stream."

In Eden, Adam and Eve knew this—no fear of tomorrow, no regret for yesterday. Revelation 10:6 (ESV) declares "no more delay" in God's realm, hinting at Eden's timeless peace. Eden was such a haven—its peace was a gift from a God beyond time's chains.

Why does understanding time and eternity matter for Christian living? Grasping God's eternal now shapes how we navigate chronos's (χρόνος, sequential time) pressures. By anchoring our lives in kairos (καιρός, God's appointed moment), we prioritize eternal values—loving God and others—over fleeting pursuits (Matthew 22:37–39, ESV). This perspective frees us from anxiety over time's limits, empowering us to steward each moment for God's glory, whether in work, relationships, or worship, trusting that our lives echo His eternal purposes (Colossians 3:17, ESV).

Is Time God's Gift?

Some argue time is God's creation—a good framework for life. Genesis 1:14's "lights... for seasons" (ESV) suggests time orders creation's purpose, they say. Calvin (1559) viewed time as a stage for glorifying God through work and love, a divine gift for stewardship. Dispensationalists like Scofield (1917) see time as the scaffolding of God's plan, each "day" a step toward redemption.

Yet mo'ed (מוֹעֵד, sacred times or divine appointments) means sacred moments, not hours, as Basil taught. Eden had no clocks—only God's river of peace. My friend Nick, a man of bold faith, once drew me into a conversation that unveiled kairos's (καιρός, God's appointed moment) power. During a long drive, we spoke over the phone about heaven, and his words were so vivid that it felt like we were together in person. Hours seemed to vanish, revealing the pull of God's eternal now. Genesis 3:8 (ESV) shows Adam and Eve walking with God, unbound by time—a kairos (καιρός, God's appointed moment) intimacy, not chronos's (χρόνος, sequential time) march.

If time were a gift, why does chronos (χρόνος, sequential time) bring loss, while kairos (καιρός, God's appointed moment) restores peace? If a heavenly rebellion sparked chronos (χρόνος, sequential time), as Chapter 2 will explore, then Eden's song stood fragile—its harmony poised to break.

Tasting Eden Today

Eden's peace isn't lost. You can touch kairos (καιρός, God's appointed moment) now.

Pause for a moment. Close your eyes and pray, "Lord, let me rest in Your now." Picture a river of God's peace washing away chronos's (χρόνος, sequential time) rush (Psalm 46:10, ESV). Recall a moment when time seemed to fade—perhaps in worship, serving others, or a quiet act of love—and let God's presence draw near. Practically, carve out daily time for Scripture and prayer to align your heart with God's purposes, and stay open to unexpected kairos (καιρός, God's appointed moment) moments.

Recently, I met a woman I knew through FCA; her husband, recovering from strokes, radiated a joy that revealed God's eternal now breaking through chronos (χρόνος, sequential time). Such moments—like a conversation that uplifts a friend or stranger or a chance to share your faith—echo Eden's timeless peace, reminding us we were made for His presence, not chronos's (χρόνος, sequential time) ticking weight (Ecclesiastes 3:11, ESV).

Such moments echo Eden, reminding us we were made for His eternal now—not for time's ticking weight.

As we turn to Chapter 2, we restate our central question: Did God create time, or did sin's echo start its countdown? We'll explore whether a cosmic fracture, born of angelic pride, cast the first shadow over paradise, disrupting Eden's timeless peace (Isaiah 14:12–15, ESV).

Chapter 2

The Fall Before the Fall

I magine eternity as a mirror—radiant and whole—reflecting God's timeless now. Then, a crack: Lucifer's pride shattered it, scattering the shards of chronos (χρόνος, sequential time)—the ticking curse of loss. Chapter 1 unveiled Eden's river of kairos (καιρός, God's eternal moment), where God's presence reigned (Genesis 2:15, ESV). But a shadow fell earlier, in heaven's heart. This chapter dares to ask: Did an angel's rebellion start time's clock, casting a fracture over paradise before Eden bloomed?

Heaven's Fracture

Isaiah 14:12-14 (ESV) mourns a fall: "How you have fallen, morning star! ... I will ascend above the stars of God." Ezekiel 28:15-17 (ESV) adds,

"Wickedness was found in you." While some interpret these verses as describing human kings, many—like Irenaeus (c. 180)—see Lucifer's pride disrupting creation's unity (Against Heresies, 5.24). Revelation 12:7-9 (ESV) glimpses a heavenly war, Satan cast down before Eden's light. His "I will" shattered God's now, birthing chronos (χρόνος, sequential time)—time's relentless march of decay. Augustine (397-400) taught that God's eternity holds all as one (Confessions, Book XI). Lucifer's defiance drew a line—before and after—scattering eternity into moments of loss.

Growing up, I'd hear my father pray, his voice steady, seeking God's eternal presence. "The Lord's forever," he'd say after, "beyond any clock." His faith pointed to a wholeness before any fracture—a heaven untouched by time. Yet that wholeness cracked, casting a shadow toward Eden.

Eden's Shadow

This heavenly crack echoed in Eden. Genesis 1's light was God's answer to chaos, not time's beginning (Genesis 1:3, ESV). Philo (c. 20-50 CE) saw creation's days as divine order, countering a prior rift (On the Creation of the World, Sections 1–3). Lewis (1940) called our world a "time-stream," pulling us from God. That stream, I believe, began in heaven. Eden's kairos (καιρός, God's eternal moment), as Chapter 1 showed, was a gift—its peace perfect. But the serpent, carrying Lucifer's echo, slithered in (Genesis 3:1, ESV), making Eden fragile—a paradise beside a fault line, vulnerable to the pre-existing heavenly rift.

Robert Marshall's near-death vision of a timeless heaven, free of clocks, recalled this lost unity (Kay, 2025). Genesis 5:24 (ESV) reveals Enoch walked so closely with God that he was taken without tasting death, suggesting he experienced a glimpse of pre-fracture wholeness—a life immersed in kairos (καιρός, God's eternal moment), unmarred by chronos's (χρόνος, sequential time) decay. If Lucifer's pride, as Irenaeus suggests, fractured God's now, it cast a shadow over creation, waiting to deepen.

Did Time Begin at Creation?

Some argue time began with Genesis 1:1 (ESV)—"In the beginning"—as a divine gift for order. The Hebrew bereshit (בְּרֵאשִׁית, in the beginning) marks a start, they say, and "seasons" (mo'ed [מוֹעֵד, appointed times]) confirm time's goodness (Genesis 1:14, ESV). Others, like Aquinas (1265-1273), see time as a neutral framework for God's plan, not a curse (Summa Theologiae, I.10).

Yet bereshit (בְּרֵאשִׁית, in the beginning) signals God's creative act—not a clock—as Rashi (c. 1100) observed (Commentary on Genesis). Mo'ed (מוֹעֵד, appointed times) means worship, not hours, as Basil of Caesarea (c. 370) taught (Hexaemeron). Ezekiel 28:13 (ESV) mentions a pre-Eden "Eden," hinting at a rupture before Earth. My father's prayers showed me God's now flows beyond chronos's (χρόνος, sequential time) shards—as Genesis 3:8's (ESV) timeless walks with God reveal. Romans 5:12 (ESV) teaches that sin introduced death into the world through Adam, and death presupposes chronos (χρόνος, sequential time), as decay requires a temporal sequence. If Lucifer's pride sparked chronos's (χρόνος, sequential time) necessity in heaven, Adam's fall widened its curse on Earth.

Seeking Kairos Today

The fracture of chronos (χρόνος, sequential time) need not bind us. You can glimpse kairos (καιρός, God's eternal moment) now. Pause and whisper, "Lord, heal time's cracks with Your now." Picture a mirror of eternity—its shards gathered by God's light. Reflect on a moment when His presence felt near—perhaps in prayer or love or meeting a stranger—and let kairos (καιρός, God's eternal moment) mend your heart. Such glimpses echo heaven's wholeness, calling us beyond chronos's (χρόνος, sequential time) weight.

As we turn to Chapter 3, we restate our question: Did time begin as a divine design—or as a fracture that only Christ can heal?

Chapter 3

Six Days or Six Stages?

Imagine creation as a painting—God's brush-strokes shaping beauty and order, not a stopwatch counting hours. Chapter 2 traced chronos (χρόνος, sequential time) to Lucifer's rebellion, a crack in eternity's mirror (Ezekiel 28:15-17, ESV). When God said, "Let there be light" (Genesis 1:3, ESV), was He starting time—or healing pride's chaos? This chapter explores Genesis 1's "days" as kairos (καιρός, God's eternal moment)—not clocks, but rhythms where God's now pulsed through a harmonious creation. Were they literal hours or sacred stages?

Creation's Song

Genesis 1's days don't tick; they sing. The Hebrew yom (,יוֹם day) can mean a 24-hour day, an age, or a divine act. Rashi (c. 1100) saw these days as declarations of purpose, not hours. No sun or moon shone until Day Four (Genesis 1:14, ESV), so God's light alone marked "evening and morning" (Genesis 1:5, ESV)—a rhythm of worship, not schedules. The Spirit hovered over chaos (Genesis 1:2, ESV), and from that void, God painted order. Psalm 104:30 (ESV) declares, "You send forth your Spirit, they are created"—a timeless act, not a timestamp.

The "lights" were for "signs and seasons" (mo'ed [,מוֹעֵד appointed times]) (Genesis 1:14, ESV)—holy feasts, not calendars, as Basil of Caesarea taught (Basil of Caesarea, c. 370). Adam and Eve lived this harmony, tending a garden without decay (Genesis 2:15, ESV). Their days were kairos (καιρός, God's eternal moment), a song of God's now.

Hearing a podcast about Robert Marshall's near-death vision, where heaven held no clocks, I felt creation's song. That story stirred my heart, revealing a rhythm beyond chronos's (χρόνος, sequential time) weight, echoing Eden's peace. Yet a crack threatened this song, waiting to break its melody.

The Fall's Shadow

Lucifer's pride, as Chapter 2 proposed, birthed chronos (χρόνος, sequential time). Genesis 1 can be viewed as God's response to rebellion—a canvas of order painted over chaos. While Scripture doesn't explicitly link Lucifer's fall to the creation narrative, many theologians have seen Genesis 1 as God's act of re-establishing harmony. But sin struck. The serpent's whisper marred the masterpiece, turning rhythm into routine (Genesis 3:1, ESV). Work became toil; death, a deadline (Genesis 3:19, ESV). Lewis (1940) called this the "time stream," pulling us from God's now. Revelation 21:23 (ESV) envisions restoration: a city needing "no sun or moon"—no clocks, only kairos (καιρός, God's eternal moment).

Enoch, who "walked with God, and he was not, for God took him" (Genesis 5:24, ESV), may have known this timeless song—a life so aligned with God's presence that he bypassed death altogether. His story hints at kairos interrupting chronos as if God lifted him beyond the time stream. Genesis 1 wasn't time's beginning but a divine act of restoring order over a fault line carved by pride.

For immortal beings—like angels or glorified saints—time may not unfold as a sequence of past, present, and future. Aquinas (1265-1273) argued that angels "understand by a single, indivisible act" (Summa Theologiae, I.58.2), not through step-by-step reasoning. They perceive truth instantly, as a whole, not in a timeline of events. Scripture offers glimpses of this: when the angel Gabriel appears to Mary in Luke 1, his message is direct, purposeful, and untouched by hesitation—as if arriving from a realm beyond delay. If Lucifer's rebellion disrupted this fullness, then the emergence of chronos marked a fall from unity into fragmentation—a descent from eternal presence into measured sequence.

Is Time a Created Good?

Some see time as God's gift. Genesis 1:14's "seasons" and 1:31's "very good" (ESV) suggest time orders creation, say dispensationalists like Scofield (1917). Aquinas (1265-1273) viewed time as a neutral framework for God's plan (Summa Theologiae, I.10). Yet mo'ed (מוֹעֵד, appointed times) means sacred moments, not hours, as Basil taught. Augustine (397-400) tied time to change, not God's eternity (Confessions, Book XI). Genesis 3:8 (ESV) shows Adam and Eve's timeless walks with God—kairos (καιρός, God's eternal moment), not chronos (χρόνος, sequential time). Reflecting on Marshall's vision, I saw heaven's rhythm, not time's march. If chronos (χρόνος, sequential time) began with Lucifer's fall, Genesis 1 was order painted over chaos, not a clock's launch.

Living Kairos Today

Eden's song isn't lost. You can hear kairos (καιρός, God's eternal moment) now. Pause and pray, "Lord, paint my heart with Your now." Picture God's brushstrokes shaping peace over your chaos. Recall a moment when His presence sang—perhaps in worship or love—and let kairos (καιρός, God's eternal moment) fill you. Such moments echo creation's rhythm, calling us beyond chronos's (χρόνος, sequential time) weight.

As we turn to Chapter 4, we'll ask: What happened when immortal beings touched time's curse?

Chapter 4

Eden's Forever

Picture Eden as a garden of forever, its blooms untouched by death's ticking clock. Chapter 3 revealed Genesis 1's days as divine brushstrokes—painting kairos (καιρός, God's eternal moment) over chaos (Genesis 1:5, ESV). Adam and Eve were created for that timeless peace, not the rush of chronos (χρόνος, sequential time). Yet, as Chapter 2 explained, an angelic rebellion had already cast a shadow over eternity (Ezekiel 28:15-17, ESV). This chapter asks: If Adam and Eve were immortal, was time ever meant for them at all?

Eden's Forever

Genesis 2:17 (ESV) warned, "In the day you eat of it, you shall surely die." Death was no part of God's original design—it was a consequence, not a feature. The Tree of Life stood as a promise of unending communion with the Creator (Genesis 2:9; 3:22, ESV). Irenaeus (c. 180) wrote that humanity was made for eternal fellowship with God, not decay (Against Heresies, Book V). Adam and Eve named the animals, tended the garden, and lived in peace, not pressure (Genesis 2:15, ESV). Their days echoed John 10:10 (ESV): "I came that they may have life and have it abundantly." Their walks with God in the "cool of the day" (Genesis 3:8, ESV) weren't scheduled—they were saturated in kairos (καιρός, God's eternal moment).

In 2025, I watched a podcast by Kay (2025), where his guest described a near-death experience of encountering God in a realm beyond time—timeless, weightless, and free from clocks. His words stirred something deep in me. I saw Eden more clearly: not just a garden, but a rhythm of being. Adam and Eve didn't manage minutes—they lived in God's presence, immersed in the kairos (καιρός, God's eternal moment), untouched by the demands of chronos.

The Fall's Clock

When Adam and Eve disobeyed, a clock began ticking. Mortality crept in—not as instant death, but as inevitable decay (Genesis 3:22-24, ESV). Work became toil. Life became loss. Gregory of Nyssa (4th century) described humanity's pre-Fall condition as angelic—free from the corruption and pressure of time (On the Soul and the Resurrection). Revelation 21:4 (ESV) envisions a return to that state: "No more death or mourning or crying or pain." Sin shattered God's eternal now. Enoch, taken without dying (Genesis 5:24, ESV), may have retained some remnant of that timeless peace. But for the rest of humanity, chronos (χρόνος, sequential time) took hold—a curse God never intended.

Does Purpose Need Time?

Some argue that time was necessary for Adam and Eve to fulfill their purpose. Calvin (1559) described creation as a theater of God's glory, where human work and love reflect divine beauty (Institutes of the Christian Religion, Book I, Chapter V). Aquinas (1265-1273) saw time as a neutral medium in which humans grow in virtue (Summa Theologiae, I.10). But Genesis 3:8 (ESV) reveals that their intimacy with God needed no schedule. Jesus Himself defined eternal life not as endless duration but as a relationship: "that they know you, the only true God" (John 17:3, ESV). Purpose was rooted in presence, not progression—in kairos, not chronos.

Reflecting on Kay's podcast, I saw more clearly that Eden's purpose wasn't rooted in the passage of time. It was rooted in presence. If chronos (χρόνος, sequential time) began with Lucifer's rebellion, as earlier chapters proposed, then Adam's sin sealed its grip on humanity. While Romans 5:12 addresses Adam specifically—"sin came into the world through one man, and death through sin"—the fracture had already begun in the heavenlies. Adam's fall made that fracture ours.

Embracing Kairos Today

Eden's forever isn't lost. You can touch kairos (καιρός, God's eternal moment) even now.

Pause and pray: "Lord, root me in Your eternal garden." Picture Eden's blooms, their stillness pushing back the noise of chronos (χρόνος, sequential time). Remember a moment when God's presence felt near—in prayer, in worship, or in love—and let kairos (καιρός, God's eternal moment) flood your heart.

Such moments echo Eden's immortality. They pull us back into rhythm with God's eternal now. As we turn to Chapter 5, we'll ask: How did the Fall's clock reshape humanity's days?

Chapter 5

When the Clock Started Ticking

Picture Eden as a garden of peace, its paths free from time's restless rush. Chapter 4 showed Adam and Eve created for forever, dwelling in *kairos* (καιρός, God's eternal moment) (Genesis 2:17, ESV). But their choice shattered this peace, chaining Eden to *chronos* (χρόνος, sequential time)—a curse of toil and death. Building on Chapter 2's cosmic fracture, this chapter asks: **How did the Fall start time's relentless countdown?**

Eden's Peace

Before sin, Eden knew no decay. Adam and Eve walked with God, their days unhurried, their hearts unbound (Genesis 3:8, ESV). There was no aging, no deadlines—just God's now. Genesis 2:15 (ESV) paints their life: tending a garden in harmony, not haste. Irenaeus (c. 180) saw humanity as made for eternal communion, not corruption. Their peace was *kairos* (καιρός, God's eternal moment)—a timeless gift.

As a boy, I'd hear my father sing Scripture by the fireplace, his voice warm with faith. "The Lord's word," he'd hum, weaving verses like Micah 6:8 (ESV) into melody, "lives beyond time." Those songs felt like Eden's peace—a glimpse of life before time's weight. But a shadow—sin's choice—broke this harmony, setting the clock in motion.

Time's Curse

Sin shattered Eden. "By the sweat of your brow, you will eat... until you return to the ground" (Genesis 3:17, 19, ESV). Death entered, *chronos* (χρόνος, sequential time) began—work became toil, and hope turned to worry. Ecclesiastes 3:1-11 (ESV) mourns, "A time for everything... yet all is vanity." Psalm 90:10

(ESV) laments, "Our years are seventy... soon gone." Yet mercy shines: "His mercies are new every morning" (Lamentations 3:22-23, ESV).

Cain's curse—to become "a fugitive and a wanderer on the earth" (Genesis 4:12, ESV)—embodied the ache of chronos. His restlessness wasn't just physical; it was temporal. Separated from God's presence, Cain drifted through time without anchoring purpose. This wandering mirrors our own experience of chronos: motion without meaning, time without peace. Athanasius (4th century) described sin as the corruption that pulls humanity away from God's eternal image. The cosmic fracture began with Lucifer, as described in Chapter 2, but Adam's and Cain's choices widened the gap—anchoring humanity in a timeline God never intended.

Is Time a Created Good?

Some argue that time was part of God's good design. Genesis 1:5's "evening and morning" suggests structure and rhythm, as highlighted in Scofield's (1917) notes on creation. Aquinas (1265-1273) described time as a neutral framework that enables moral development (Summa Theologiae). But the Hebrew word *mo'ed* (—)מֹועֵד used in Genesis 1:14—means appointed times, not rigid hours. Basil of Caesarea (c. 370) emphasized these as sacred rhythms, not mechanical measurements. Genesis 2:15 (ESV) shows Eden's harmony—unhurried, unstained by decay. It was not time that fractured Eden, but sin.

My father's Scripture songs carried *kairos's* (καιρός, God's eternal moment) echo, and Lamentations 3:22-23 (ESV) reminds us that God's mercies are new every morning—renewal beyond *chronos's* (χρόνος, sequential time) curse. If an angelic rebellion sparked *chronos* (χρόνος, sequential time), the Fall locked us into its countdown. But that was never God's intent.

Finding Kairos Today

Time's curse need not bind us. You can touch *kairos* (καιρός, God's eternal moment) now.

Pause and pray, "Lord, free me from time's chains with Your now." Picture Eden's garden, its peace washing away *chronos's* (χρόνος, sequential time) rush. Recall a moment when God's word sang in your heart—perhaps in Scripture or worship—and let *kairos* (καιρός, God's eternal moment) renew you.

Such moments echo Eden's peace, calling us beyond time's curse. As we turn to Chapter 6, we'll ask: **How did Christ's coming shatter time's curse to restore God's eternal now?**

Chapter 6

Kairos Made Flesh

Imagine Jesus as light breaking through time's fog, scattering the shadows of chronos (χρόνος, sequential time). Chapter 5 showed how sin chained humanity to chronos's (χρόνος, sequential time) curse of toil and death (Genesis 3:19, ESV). But eternity stepped in. Jesus, God's eternal now, entered our fractured world, bringing kairos (καιρός, God's eternal moment). This chapter explores how Christ's life shattered time's grip, restoring Eden's forever.

Christ's Kairos

The Fall trapped us in chronos (χρόνος, sequential time), but Jesus was unbound. He was kairos (καιρός, God's eternal moment) made flesh—fully God, fully man. "Before Abraham was, I am" (John 8:58, ESV), He declared—timeless in a world of clocks. His ministry echoed this: "The hour is coming, and is now here"—when worship transcends time (John 4:23, ESV). Athanasius (4th century) described Christ's incarnation as God's now entering history (On the Incarnation). Every act of Jesus pointed to eternity—not a better now, but a restored forever.

I once heard a speaker proclaim that Jesus' love unites all people—beyond culture, language, or time. His words—that Christ died for everyone—stirred my heart as if Jesus' eternal presence stood before me.

Miracles of Now

Christ's miracles weren't mere signs—they were eruptions of kairos (καιρός, God's eternal moment). When He healed Bartimaeus (Mark 10:46-52, ESV), raised Jairus's daughter (Mark 5:21-43, ESV), or calmed the storm

(Mark 4:39, ESV), chronos (χρόνος, sequential time) cracked. The leper's skin cleared instantly (Mark 1:40-42, ESV). The paralytic walked at once (Mark 2:1-12, ESV). These were not anomalies—they were Eden restored, if only for a moment.

When He raised Lazarus (John 11:43-44, ESV), eternity shone through death's veil, echoing the podcast's truth about Christ's timeless love (Kay, 2025). Each miracle was a declaration: God's now still reigns.

Beyond Time's Veil

After His resurrection, Jesus moved through walls (John 20:19, ESV), appeared suddenly (Luke 24:36, ESV), and vanished (Luke 24:31, ESV). He ascended beyond sight (Acts 1:9, ESV), unbound by chronos (χρόνος, sequential time). To the thief on the cross, He promised, "Today you will be with me in paradise" (Luke 23:43, ESV)—a kairos (καιρός, God's eternal moment), not a calendar.

He prayed, "This is eternal life: to know You" (John 17:3, ESV), defining forever not as infinite minutes but as presence. The Transfiguration unveiled His glory in a kairos (καιρός, God's eternal moment) moment, where time faded and eternity flashed (Matthew 17:1-8, ESV).

Are Miracles Just Anomalies?

Bultmann (1941) viewed miracles as symbolic stories for spiritual truths rather than historical events (New Testament and Mythology). Aquinas (1265-1273) saw miracles as acts above nature, not against it—signs of God's direct action in creation (Summa Theologiae). Lewis (1947) called them 'windows' into the eternal—God's signature interrupting the natural order with divine presence (Miracles).

The podcast's message of Christ's universal love echoed this: miracles like Lazarus's raising (John 11:43-44, ESV; Kay, 2025) break chronos's (χρόνος, sequential time) curse. John 17:3 (ESV) reminds us that eternal life is not endless time—it is knowing God.

If sin introduced chronos (χρόνος, sequential time), Christ's life—and miracles—proclaim kairos (καιρός, God's eternal moment) restored. His resurrection is not just hope for the future but a victory that reaches backward and forward through all of time: "Death is swallowed up in victory" (1 Corinthians 15:54-55, ESV).

Living Kairos Today

Christ's kairos (καιρός, God's eternal moment) is ours to touch.

Pause and pray: "Lord, let Your light break through my time." Picture Jesus as light, scattering chronos's (χρόνος, sequential time) fog. Recall a moment when His love felt near—perhaps in worship, in Scripture, or in grace—and let kairos (καιρός, God's eternal moment) renew you.

Such moments echo Eden's forever, calling us beyond time's curse. As we turn to Chapter 7, we'll ask: How did Christ's cross and resurrection redeem time's brokenness?

Chapter 7

Time as a Divine Concession

Picture time as a bridge God built—not our home, but a path back to His eternal shore. Chapter 6 revealed Jesus as kairos (καιρός, God's eternal moment), breaking the curse of chronos (χρόνος, sequential time) (John 8:58, ESV). If the Fall trapped us in chronos (χρόνος, sequential time), as Chapter 5 explained, why didn't God end time? Because even judgment holds mercy. In one theological view, time is not God's original design but a redemptive concession—a framework through which God holds space for salvation. What was fractured by sin, God now uses for healing. Time, then, becomes not a home but a bridge.

When Jesus rose from the tomb (John 20:19, ESV), eternity pierced time—a kairos (καιρός,

God's eternal moment) moment echoing God's redemptive plan. This chapter explores time as His mercy: a bridge guiding us home through divine breaches.

Time's Mercy

Galatians 4:4 (ESV) declares, "When the fullness of time had come, God sent His Son." Time is not praised—it is a stage for salvation. After the Fall, God gave structures—Sabbaths (Exodus 20:8-11, ESV), feasts (Leviticus 23, ESV), and prophecies (Daniel 9:24-27, ESV)—to hold space until Christ. These were not countdowns—they were mercies. Gregory of Nazianzus (4th century) saw God entering time to break its grip. Time is a bridge—not a home.

As a boy, I remember my father teaching me about redemption, his eyes bright with hope. "God's mercy," he said, "builds a path through time to His forever." That truth felt like crossing a bridge to Eden's shore—where chronos (χρόνος, sequential time) fades. However, God's plan went further still: to make time a passage to salvation.

Kairos Breaches

The Sabbath interrupts chronos (χρόνος, sequential time), not merely by pausing activity but by realigning us with God's rhythm. It's not just rest—it's resistance. Each Sabbath is a kairos invitation: to cease striving, to remember Eden, and to preview eternity. Hebrews 4:9 (ESV) calls it a "Sabbath rest for the people of God"—not a break in the week, but a breach in time. Maximus the Confessor (7th century) called such moments 'divine interruptions'—eternity invading history to realign it with God's will. The cross was not merely a moment in time but time's turning point—where kairos overwhelmed chronos.

These weren't time's triumphs—they were its unraveling. Genesis 1's first kairos (καιρός, God's eternal moment) (Genesis 1:5, ESV) whispered this rhythm; the cross shouted it. Revelation 21:23-25 (ESV) envisions a city with "no sun or moon," where God's presence dissolves time's need. The end of chronos (χρόνος, sequential time) is not destruction—it is restoration.

Is Time Redemptively Good?

Some argue time is a divine gift. Calvin (1559) viewed time as a stewardship gift, allowing creation to glorify God through ordered existence (Institutes of the Christian Religion). Scofield (1917) described time as part of God's prophetic structure. Aquinas (1265-1273) described time as neither inherently good nor evil but a medium for growth (Summa Theologiae).

But God also used exile and crucifixion—neither ideal—as instruments of redemption. Like them, time is a tool—not a treasure. Basil of Caesarea (c. 370) noted that the Hebrew term mo'ed (מוֹעֵד)refers to sacred appointments—moments of encounter, not mechanisms of control. My father's words echoed this:

Redemption flows from kairos (καιρός, God's eternal moment), not the march of chronos (χρόνος, sequential time). Galatians 4:4's (ESV) "fullness" was not about time's perfection—but eternity's breakthrough.

Crossing Time's Bridge Today

Time's bridge leads to kairos (καιρός, God's eternal moment)—and you can walk it now.

Pause and pray: "Lord, guide me across time to Your forever." Picture a bridge spanning chronos's (χρόνος, sequential time) restless rush, leading to God's shore. Recall a moment when His mercy felt near—perhaps in rest, grace, or quiet faithfulness—and let kairos (καιρός, God's eternal moment) renew you.

Such moments echo Eden's forever. They remind us that time was never the goal—but the way back. As we turn to Chapter 8, we'll ask: How will Christ's return restore eternity's fullness?

Chapter 8

Eternity's Tapestry

Picture Christ weaving time's fragile threads into eternity's tapestry. Chapter 7 shows time as a bridge—a divine concession for redemption (Galatians 4:4, ESV). In Jesus, that bridge reached its shore. His coming was the fullness of time—kairos (καιρός, God's eternal moment)—gathering the shattered pieces of chronos (χρόνος, sequential time). This chapter celebrates how Christ's life didn't just interrupt time—it wove eternity back into our world.

Christ's Fullness

Galatians 4:4 (ESV) declares, "When the fullness of time had come, God sent His Son." This was not time's triumph—it was kairos (καιρός, God's eternal moment) breaking through.

Prophecies pointed to Him: Isaiah's virgin birth (Isaiah 7:14, ESV), Micah's Bethlehem (Micah 5:2, ESV), and Daniel's "seventy weeks" leading to redemption (Daniel 9:24-27, ESV). Jesus was eternity's heart, uniting "all things in Him, things in heaven and on earth" (Ephesians 1:10, ESV)—reconciling relationships and creation and restoring the very order of time. In Him, fragmented chronos are gathered and fulfilled. What sin scattered, Christ gathers—healing even the rhythm of history.

Irenaeus (c. 180) saw Christ as the head of a renewed creation, restoring what sin had fractured. In worship one morning, singing of Christ's love, I felt time dissolve. His presence stitched my fleeting moments into something eternal—each one a thread drawn into a greater design. Heaven's tapestry brushed earth that morning. That moment was kairos—God weaving time and eternity into one seamless story. That was kairos (καιρός, God's eternal moment)—God's now, uniting all.

And yet, Christ's life was more than a glimpse. It was eternity's fullness in the flesh.

Time's Gathering

Christ's birth, life, death, and resurrection gathered time's threads. The cross was the ultimate kairos (καιρός, God's eternal moment)—where sin's curse met God's love (1 Corinthians 15:54-55, ESV). In worship today, the church carries this fullness: "The hour is now here" (John 4:23-24, ESV). In sacraments, prayer, and feasts, chronos (χρόνος, sequential time) is cracked open. Maximus the Confessor (7th century) described these moments as divine irruptions—where eternity breaks in.

Revelation 10:6 (ESV) declares, "There would be no more delay," signaling the fulfillment of God's redemptive plan—not the elimination of time itself, but the end of waiting. In the new creation, God's presence replaces delay. Time gives way to immediacy, to kairos realized fully.

Is Time a Permanent Good?

Some see time as God's enduring gift. Keller (2011) describes it as a rhythm for glorifying God through meaningful work and love. Aquinas (1265-1273) saw time as a neutral framework enabling growth (Summa Theologiae). But Augustine (397-400) called time a shadow—a moving image far from God's stillness (Confessions).

That moment of worship—when Christ's presence outshone the clock—confirmed it: We do not need time to encounter eternity. "The hour is now here" (John 4:23-24, ESV). If sin introduced chronos (χρόνος, sequential time), then Christ's coming fulfilled its purpose. And Revelation 21:23 (ESV) envisions a city that needs no sun or moon—for the Lamb is its light.

Time as we know it—bound to decay, waiting, and separation—will end. What remains is not a void but a redeemed presence: eternity. Chronos will be transformed, not discarded, as kairos become all-encompassing. In God's city, time is no longer needed to mark distance, for the Lamb is near (Revelation 21:23, ESV).

Weaving Eternity Today

Christ's kairos (καιρός, God's eternal moment) is ours to touch.

Pause and pray: "Lord, weave my time into Your eternity." Picture Christ's love as a thread, binding your fragile hours to His forever. Recall a moment when His presence felt near—perhaps in worship, silence, or grace—and let kairos (καιρός, God's eternal moment) renew you.

Such moments echo eternity's tapestry, calling us beyond time's curse. As we turn to Chapter 9, we'll ask: How can we live in Christ's kairos daily?

Chapter 9

Windows to Eternity

Imagine kairos (καιρός, God's eternal moment) as a window to eternity—open, even in time's fog. Chapter 8 celebrated Christ's fullness, weaving the threads of chronos (χρόνος, sequential time) into God's now (Galatians 4:4, ESV). We are called to live there—to worship, love, and serve not in the rush of chronos (χρόνος, sequential time) but in the peace of kairos (καιρός, God's eternal moment). This chapter urges us to redeem time's curse by embracing His eternal now.

Kairos Living

Jesus said, "The hour is now here when true worshipers will worship the Father in spirit and truth" (John 4:23-24, ESV). Worship cracks open time. The Eucharist and baptism—rooted in Christ's eternal fullness (1 Corinthians 10:16, ESV)—are kairos (καιρός, God's eternal moment) moments that unite us to eternity. Maximus the Confessor (7th century) described such acts as joining God's now. Even daily love fulfills this call: "Whatever you do... do everything in the name of the Lord Jesus" (Colossians 3:17, ESV).

Even chores can become kairos (καιρός, God's eternal moment)—when done in love, gratitude, and presence. We sanctify the ordinary by washing dishes while praying for your family, folding laundry with joy, or preparing a meal with thankfulness. When our posture shifts from obligation to offering, the moment becomes eternal. As Lawrence (17th century) described in *The Practice of the Presence of God*, even peeling potatoes can become worship.

In a quiet prayer one morning, seeking God's presence, I felt chronos (χρόνος, sequential time) fade. His peace opened a window to eternity as heaven's light poured through the moment. That was kairos (καιρός, God's eternal moment)—God's now, breaking into the ordinary. Christ invites us to live like this daily, redeeming time's rhythm with His presence.

Piercing Time

The church's rhythms—prayer, sacrifice, and service—echo Eden's peace (Chapter 1). Hebrews 13:15-16 (ESV) urges us to "offer a sacrifice of praise" and to "not neglect to do good." These simple acts pierce time's fog. Gregory of Nyssa (4th century) taught that eternity begins now—in the presence of God. Revelation 22:5 (ESV) envisions a city where "night will be no more"—not as the end of time itself, but as the end of fear, separation, and delay. The verse speaks of divine illumination: "They will need no light of lamp or sun, for the Lord God will be their light." In that light, kairos (καιρός, God's eternal moment) becomes the only rhythm, and chronos (χρόνος, sequential time) fades in significance.

Basil of Caesarea (c. 370) linked worship to mo'ed (מוֹעֵד, appointed times), not to ticking clocks. Through worship, we live redeemed—still moving through chronos (χρόνος, sequential time) but no longer ruled by it. We live in time, but our purpose, peace, and identity are anchored in kairos (καιρός, God's eternal moment). The Spirit enables us to live forward while rooted in eternity—walking in rhythms of grace, not deadlines.

Is Chronos Necessary for Growth?

Some argue that chronos (χρόνος, sequential time) is essential for spiritual maturity. Wimber (1986) saw prayer, fasting, and healing as rhythms rooted in time. Aquinas (1265-1273) also viewed time as neutral—a framework for growth (Summa Theologiae). However, Augustine (397-400) called time a shadow, not part of God's original design (Confessions).

That quiet prayer, where God's presence outshone the ticking of hours, echoed Augustine's claim. Kairos (καιρός, God's eternal moment) moments don't bypass growth—they fulfill it. They are the lived expression of Hebrews 13:15-16 (ESV): doing good, offering praise, and thriving in eternity's rhythm. If sin shaped chronos (χρόνος, sequential time), Christ's kairos (καιρός, God's eternal moment) frees us to live fully now (John 4:23-24, ESV).

Living Through Kairos Today

Christ's kairos (καιρός, God's eternal moment) is yours to embrace.

Pause and pray: "Lord, open a window to eternity in me." Picture His presence as light, shining through time's fog. Recall a moment when His peace felt near—perhaps in worship, prayer, or service—and let kairos (καιρός, God's eternal moment) renew your soul.

Such moments are windows to eternity. They remind us that heaven's rhythm already pulses through our ordinary days. We don't escape time—we transform it. Through worship, service, and presence, we stitch kairos into our calendar and walk with Christ in eternity, even now.

As we turn to Chapter 10, we'll learn: How will Christ's eternal city fulfill our kairos living forever?

Chapter 10

The Ocean of Eternity

Picture chronos (χρόνος, sequential time) as a river—narrow, restless, winding—flowing into the boundless ocean of kairos (καιρός, God's eternal moment), where all streams of time are gathered and stilled. God's presence washes over all moments in that eternal sea at once. There, the river doesn't end in loss—it expands into glory. Chapter 9 urged us to live in kairos (καιρός, God's eternal moment), piercing time's fog with worship (John 4:23-24, ESV). This book began with a question: Is time a curse? From Lucifer's rebellion (Chapter 2) to the Fall's clock (Chapter 5) to Christ's fullness (Chapter 8), we've traced time's shadow and God's answer.

This final chapter envisions our true home: a timeless heaven where chronos (χρόνος, sequential time) ends and kairos (καιρός, God's eternal moment) reigns.

Glimpses Now

Even within chronos (χρόνος, sequential time), we taste eternity. Worship, love, and prayer—as Chapter 9 showed—are kairos (καιρός, God's eternal moment) windows. Jesus prayed, "This is eternal life, that they know you, the only true God, and Jesus Christ whom you have sent" (John 17:3, ESV). Eternal life is not endless minutes but intimate communion—knowing God and His Son. That relationship is the center of kairos, where presence replaces the passage of time. Gregory of Nazianzus (4th century) described Christ's incarnation as eternity touching earth.

A pastor's sermon once painted heaven as a timeless ocean, where every moment rests in God's now. That vision stirred my soul like kairos's (καιρός, God's eternal moment) waves washed over me. These glimpses don't just comfort; they prepare us, aligning our hearts with God's forever.

Heaven's Now

Revelation 21:1-5 (ESV) promises a new heaven and a new earth: "no more death or crying." "Night will be no more" because God's light dissolves time's need (Revelation 22:5, ESV). Isaiah 65:17 (ESV) foretells a world where chronos (χρόνος, sequential time) dissolves into joy: "The former things shall not be remembered."

Maximus the Confessor (7th century) taught that eternity gathers all into God's now. We will know Him fully, just as we are fully known. 2 Peter 3:13 (ESV) awaits "a new earth where righteousness dwells." This isn't merely endless time—it is Eden restored through God's eternal presence. In the garden, Adam and Eve walked with God in uninterrupted fellowship. Heaven renews that rhythm, not through a clock but through communion. In eternity, kairos becomes the atmosphere, and God's presence is the light by which all is known.

Does Time Persist in Eternity?

Some envision time in heaven. Dispensationalists like Scofield (1917) view eternity as composed of ordered ages. Wright (2008) imagines renewed creation marked by "rhythms of joy"—not as rigid succession, but as redeemed patterns of worship, rest, and celebration (Surprised by Hope). These rhythms don't reintroduce fallen time but express divine order within God's eternal presence. It's not chronos reborn—it's kairos choreographed. Aquinas (1265-1273) described eternity as beyond succession yet permitting divine order (Summa Theologiae).

Augustine (397-400) described eternity as "God's today"—not spread across past, present, and future, but wholly present, unmeasured, and indivisible (Confessions, Book XI).

In contrast to human experience, which moves through time, God embraces all time in a single act of knowing and loving. The pastor's sermon echoed this truth: No clocks are needed in heaven. God's light shines forever (Revelation 22:5, ESV). If sin introduced chronos (χρόνος, sequential time), then Christ's kairos (καιρός, God's eternal moment) leads us to a timeless home (Revelation 21:4, ESV).

Embracing Eternity Today

Heaven's kairos (καιρός, God's eternal moment) begins now.

Pause and pray: "Lord, let Your eternal ocean wash over me." Picture chronos's (χρόνος, sequential time) river flowing into God's boundless now. Recall a moment when His eternity felt near—perhaps in worship, prayer, or love—and let kairos (καιρός, God's eternal moment) renew your soul.

These moments echo our timeless home. They remind us that eternity is not distant—it is already breaking in. Like waves from a divine ocean, kairos laps at the shores of our days, calling us to step beyond the clock and into communion. There, in God's presence, time's curse dissolves into forever joy.

The Epilogue reflects on this journey: from the curse of time to the light of forever.

Epilogue: The Eternal Now

This book began with a question: **Is time our curse, or is *kairos* our call?**

From Eden's timeless peace to a cosmic fracture, from the Fall's relentless clock to Christ's redeeming cross, I've pursued one truth: **We were not made for minutes. We were made for Jesus—our bridge into God's eternal now** (*kairos* [καιρός, God's eternal moment]).

Reflecting on the Journey

In Eden, time flowed as *mo'ed* (מוֹעֵד, appointed times), not the ticking tyranny of *chronos* (χρόνος, sequential time) (Genesis 3:8, ESV). However, a fracture loomed. Lucifer's pride shattered the mirror of eternity, unleashing *chronos's* shadow (Chapter 2). Humanity's sin deepened the fracture—"By the sweat of your face..." (Genesis 3:19, ESV).

Irenaeus (c. 180) described this as our descent from incorruptibility into corruption, from the eternal into the temporal.

Jesus—*kairos* (καιρός, God's eternal moment) made flesh—stepped into the fracture. His miracles, resurrection, and the promise, "Today you will be with me in paradise" (Luke 23:43, ESV) disrupted time's dominion (Chapter 6). In Him, *chronos* (χρόνος, sequential time) bends back toward eternity's thread (Galatians 4:4, ESV; Chapter 8).

Willard (1998) described rebellion as a distortion of divine order, a descent into futility. He wrote, "The eternal kind of life is not something waiting for us after death. It is the life we now have through interactive relationship with God" (p. 276). Salvation, then, is surrender—"to know You... this is eternal life" (John 17:3, ESV).

Along This Journey

- My father's teaching unveiled Eden's peace (Chapter 1).

- Singing Scripture opened creation's harmony (Chapter 4).

- In worship, time dissolved into God's presence (Chapter 8).

- In quiet prayer, *kairos* (καιρός, God's eternal moment) light broke through (Chapter 9).

- A pastor's sermon painted heaven's ocean of timelessness (Chapter 10).

Each was a glimpse of the eternal now, where *chronos* (χρόνος, sequential time) fades, and Jesus draws near.

Living the Eternal Now

Augustine (397-400) wrote that God's eternity is not stretched across past and future but stands as a whole: "Your 'today' is eternity... because it does not give way to tomorrow, nor does it follow yesterday." In God, all moments are present—indivisible and complete.

We taste this wholeness in every *mo'ed* (מוֹעֵד, appointed times)—acts of love, mercy, worship, obedience.

Pause and pray: "Lord, anchor me in Your eternal now." Picture *chronos* (χρόνος, sequential time) melting in *kairos's* (καιρός, God's eternal moment) warm, eternal light. Remember a moment when Jesus felt close—in silence, service, or stillness—and let His now renew your now.

Conclusion

Chronos (χρόνος, sequential time) binds, but Jesus frees. Cast your heart toward Him. Let every holy moment defy the clock. Your home is not in time—but in His eternal now, where death and clocks vanish forever (Revelation 21:4, ESV).

Bonus Chapter: Seeing with Kairos Eyes—A Guided Study of Jesus' Words

You've journeyed through chronos (χρόνος, sequential time)—its curse, weight, and fragmentation—and glimpsed kairos (καιρός, God's eternal moment), breaking in. One evening, reading John 17:3 (ESV), I felt time still. Jesus' words—"This is eternal life, that they know you"—pierced the moment. It was a mo'ed (מוֹעֵד, appointed time), where heaven touched earth.

This chapter invites you to read Scripture as holy interruptions—kairos (καιρός, God's eternal moment) bursts in chronos's (χρόνος, sequential time) fog—beckoning you to live in God's eternal now.

Pause. Reflect. Let kairos shine.

1. The Kingdom Is Here Now

Verse: "The kingdom of God is at hand; repent and believe in the gospel." — Mark 1:15 (ESV)

See Also: "The kingdom of God is in the midst of you." — Luke 17:20–21 (ESV)

Context: Jesus proclaimed the Kingdom not as a distant future but as kairos (καιρός, God's eternal moment)—breaking into their present. Yet many expected political revolution and missed the invitation to surrender now.

Reflection: Do you wait for God's Kingdom to come "someday"? What if it's already moving in your midst—in conversations, interruptions, convictions? Try praying: "Lord, let me recognize Your Kingdom now."

Holy Interruption: Kairos (καιρός, God's eternal moment) is not just near—it's within you, Jesus says. Let that reframe your now.

2. Salvation Is Today

Verse: "Truly, I say to you, today you will be with me in paradise." — Luke 23:43 (ESV)

See Also: "Whoever hears my word and believes...has passed from death to life." — John 5:24 (ESV)

Context: On the cross, Jesus didn't offer a delayed hope but immediate grace—a kairos (καιρός, God's eternal moment) rescue for the thief. Time collapsed. Heaven opened.

Reflection: Are you waiting to be "ready" for God's grace? What if today is your mo'ed (,מוֹעֵד appointed time)? Pause now. Say thank you to the One who redeems this moment.

Holy Interruption: Eternity can begin now—for you, for anyone who turns to Him.

3. Eternal Life Is Knowing Jesus Now

Verse: "This is eternal life, that they know you, the only true God, and Jesus Christ whom you have sent." — John 17:3 (ESV)

See Also: "I came that they may have life and have it abundantly." — John 10:10 (ESV)

Context: Eternal life isn't a postmortem upgrade—it's knowing God now. Many missed this kairos (καιρός, God's eternal moment) invitation, mistaking it for a promise of someday.

Reflection: Do you think of eternal life as later? Or as life with Jesus now? What's one way you can know Him today—perhaps in stillness, gratitude, or Scripture?

Holy Interruption: Jesus doesn't offer just length of life, but depth of now.

4. Seek the Kingdom First

Verse: "Seek first the kingdom of God and his righteousness, and all these things will be added to you." — Matthew 6:33 (ESV)

See Also: "Do not be anxious about tomorrow." — Matthew 6:34 (ESV)

Context: Speaking to chronos (χρόνος, sequential time) anxieties—food, clothing, time—Jesus redirected attention toward the kairos (καιρός, God's eternal moment) priority: God's Kingdom now. Willard (1998) wrote, "When we seek the Kingdom, we live from eternity now" (p. 276).

Reflection: What worries dominate your schedule? What if kairos (καιρός, God's eternal moment) priorities re-ordered your calendar? Name one Kingdom thing to do today.

Holy Interruption: Seeking first is not about sequence—it's about orientation. Let eternity lead.

5. Worship in Spirit Now

Verse: "The hour is coming, and is now here, when the true worshipers will worship the Father in spirit and truth." — John 4:23 (ESV)

Context: To the Samaritan woman, Jesus revealed that worship is no longer bound by temples or chronos (χρόνος, sequential time) schedules—it is communion in kairos (καιρός, God's eternal moment). Augustine (397-400) wrote that God's eternity is "Your today," which never yields to tomorrow (Confessions). Maximus the Confessor (7th century) described worship as a ladder into divine union.

Reflection: Have you confined worship to a time or place? What would it mean to worship God right now, in spirit and truth?

Holy Interruption: Worship is your gateway to eternity. Open it now.

Living with Kairos Eyes

Jesus' words are lightning strikes in the sky of chronos (χρόνος, sequential time)—kairos (καιρός, God's eternal moment) bursts calling you to wake, trust, and live. Pray:

"Lord, give me kairos eyes to see Your eternal now."

Let His words illuminate your soul. Journal a mo'ed (,מוֹעֵד appointed time)—a sacred moment when Scripture broke through. Let it renew you today.

Worship. Let chronos fade. Live in His eternal now.

About the Author

Christian A. Dickinson is an educator, coach, leader, speaker, and thinker who sees the world through a lens shaped by Scripture and sharpened by logic. With over two decades of experience mentoring students and athletes, he brings a unique voice to the intersection of theology, time, and human experience.

Christian's writing blends personal stories with deep biblical insight, anchored in the conviction that truth must be both spiritually discerned and intellectually honest. In *The Curse of Time*, he draws from a lifelong fascination with time's mysteries, weaving together childhood moments, ancient texts, and modern thought to explore how eternity fractured—and how God still breaks through.

He lives in Florida with his wife, Morgan, and their children, where they run Learning Engineered Publishing, a faith-based company committed to truth, hope, and legacy.

More by Christian A. Dickinson

I f you enjoyed *The Curse of Time,* you may also appreciate these Christ-centered resources:

Jesus Was Funnier Than You Think: Unlocking His Wit, Wisdom, and Unexpected Humor A fresh look at the wit and humor of Jesus Christ — revealing the brilliant, joyful ways He taught truth and disarmed pride.

The Prophetic Equation: Thirty Prophets. One Christ. Zero Coincidence. An exploration of how thirty prophetic voices across centuries, kingdoms, and crises converge with stunning precision in Jesus Christ—revealing that Scripture is not random but a masterpiece of divine design.

Micah 6:8: A Prophetic Bridge to Jesus: A concise biblical commentary exploring how one ancient verse points forward to the life and ministry of Christ.

Every Tear Remembered: God's Presence in Our Grief: A reflection on sorrow, healing, and hope through the lens of God's enduring love.

It's All or Nothing: How Jesus Raised the Standard from Tithing to Full Surrender: A biblical commentary challenging traditional views of tithing by exploring Jesus' call to radical, Spirit-led generosity.

FULL CIRCLE: PREGAME — A Devotional Series for Athletes A faith-building devotional connecting sports, life, and Scripture to help athletes live with purpose and passion for Christ. Dickinson teams up with Anthony "Diso" Paradiso—his former high school quarterback and now a highly accomplished coach—to bring this powerful message full circle.

Glossary

Chronos is the Greek word for sequential, measurable time—the ticking clock of hours, days, and years. This book depicts chronos as a fallen state, a chain born of sin that pulls us from God's presence.

Eternity: God's timeless reality, where past, present, and future are one in His presence. Eternity is our true home, restored by Christ beyond the limits of chronos.

Kairos: The Greek word for God's time—eternal, perfect moments where heaven touches earth. Kairos is God's "now," free of haste or loss, as seen in Eden, Christ's miracles, and worship.

Lucifer's Rebellion: A speculative idea, drawn from *Isaiah 14* and *Ezekiel 28*, suggesting Satan's pride in heaven sparked the first fracture of eternity, introducing chronos before Eden's fall.

Mo'ed: A Hebrew word from *Genesis 1:14*, often translated as "seasons," but meaning sacred times or divine appointments. It points to worshipful rhythms, not chronological hours.

Redemption: God's act of restoring humanity and creation to eternity through Christ's life, death, and resurrection (*Galatians 4:4, Ephesians 1:10*). In this book, redemption heals the fracture of The Fall, freeing us from chronos.

Sabbath: A divinely ordained rest (*Exodus 20:8–11, Hebrews 4:9*), interrupting chronos with kairos, reflecting God's mercy and eternal rhythm. The Sabbath is a sacred mo'ed in this book, restoring creation's harmony.

The Fall: The moment Adam and Eve sinned (*Genesis 3*), bringing death and chronos into the world, breaking the timeless peace of Eden.

Worship: The act of entering God's kairos through praise, prayer, and obedience (*John 4:23–24*, *Hebrews 13:15–16*), aligning with mo'ed and eternity. In this book, worship is a timeless connection to God's presence.

Annotated Bibliography

Aquinas, T. (1265–1273). *Summa Theologiae*. Translated by the Fathers of the English Dominican Province. New York: Christian Classics, 1981.

Athanasius. (4th century). *On the Incarnation*. Translated by John Behr. Yonkers, NY: St Vladimir's Seminary Press, 2011.

Augustine. (397–400). *Confessions*. Translated by Henry Chadwick. Oxford: Oxford University Press, 1991.

Basil of Caesarea. (c. 370). *Hexaemeron*. In *Hexaemeron, Homilies on the Psalms, Homilies on the Proverbs*, translated by Agnes Clare Way. Washington, D.C.: Catholic University of America Press, 1963.

Brother Lawrence. (17th century). *The Practice of the Presence of God*. Translated by John J. Delaney. New York: Image Books, 1977.

Bultmann, R. (1941). *New Testament and Mythology and Other Basic Writings*. Translated by Schubert M. Ogden. Minneapolis: Fortress Press, 1984.

Calvin, J. (1559). *Institutes of the Christian Religion*. Translated by Ford Lewis Battles. Louisville: Westminster John Knox Press, 2006.

English Standard Version Bible. (2001). Wheaton, IL: Crossway Bibles.

Gregory of Nazianzus. (4th century). *Theological Orations*. Translated by Frederick Williams and Lionel Wickham. Crestwood, NY: St Vladimir's Seminary Press, 2002.

Gregory of Nyssa. (4th century). *On the Soul and the Resurrection*. Translated by Catherine P. Roth. Crestwood, NY: St Vladimir's Seminary Press, 1993.

Irenaeus. (c. 180). *Against Heresies*. Translated by Dominic J. Unger and John J. Dillon. New York: Paulist Press, 1992.

Kay, R. (2025, January). "I died for 44 hours & God answered the mysteries of life!" [Video]. YouTube. https://www.youtube.com/watch?v=xVxqCAmpvmw

Keller, T. (2011). *Every Good Endeavor: Connecting Your Work to God's Work*. New York: Dutton.

Lewis, C. S. (1940). *The Problem of Pain*. New York: HarperOne, 2001.

Lewis, C. S. (1947). *Miracles*. New York: HarperOne, 2001.

Lewis, C. S. (1964). *Letters to Malcolm: Chiefly on Prayer*. New York: Harcourt, Brace & World.

Maximus the Confessor. (7th century). *On Difficulties in the Church Fathers: The Ambigua*. Translated by Nicholas Constas. Cambridge, MA: Harvard University Press, 2014.

Philo of Alexandria. (c. 20–50 CE). *On the Creation*. In *The Works of Philo*, translated by C. D. Yonge. Peabody, MA: Hendrickson Publishers, 1993.

Rashi. (c. 1100). *Commentary on the Torah*. Translated by Rabbi A. M. Silverstein. New York: Mesorah Publications, 1999.

Scofield, C. I. (1917). *The Scofield Reference Bible*. New York: Oxford University Press, 1945.

Willard, D. (1998). *The Divine Conspiracy: Rediscovering Our Hidden Life in God*. San Francisco: HarperSanFrancisco.

Wimber, J. (1986). *Power Evangelism*. San Francisco: Harper & Row.

Wright, N. T. (2008). *Surprised by Hope: Rethinking Heaven, the Resurrection, and the Mission of the Church*. New York: HarperOne.

Scripture Reference Index

Micah 5:2 (ESV) – Chapter 8

Micah 6:8 (ESV) – Chapter 5

Psalm 90:2 (ESV) – Chapter 1

Psalm 90:10 (ESV) – Chapter 5

Revelation 10:6 (ESV) – Chapters 1, 8, 10

Revelation 12:7-9 (ESV) – Chapter 2

Revelation 21:1-5 (ESV) – Chapter 10

Revelation 21:4 (ESV) – Chapter 10, Epilogue

Revelation 21:23 (ESV) – Chapters 3, 8

Revelation 21:23-25 (ESV) – Chapters 6, 7

Revelation 22:5 (ESV) – Chapters 9, 10

Romans 5:12 (ESV) – Chapter 2

1 Corinthians 10:16 (ESV) – Chapter 9

1 Corinthians 15:54-55 (ESV) – Chapters 7, 8

2 Peter 3:13 (ESV) – Chapter 10